THE ADVENTURES OF DR. SLOTH

REBECCA CLIFFE
AND HER **QUEST**
TO PROTECT **SLOTHS**

WRITTEN AND PHOTOGRAPHED BY
SUZI ESZTERHAS

M Millbrook Press / Minneapolis

THiS BOOK iS DEDiCATED TO BECKy. THANK YOU
FOR YOUR FRiENDSHiP AND OUR ADVENTURES.

Millbrook Press™
An imprint of Lerner Publishing Group, Inc.
241 First Avenue North
Minneapolis, MN 55401 USA

For reading levels and more information, look up this title at www.lernerbooks.com.

Additional images: photo courtesy of the Sloth Conservation Foundation, pp. 6, 7, 19, 24, 25 (top right),
28, 31 (top right); Imagebroker/Alamy Stock Photo, p. 10 (bottom).
Map on p. 11 by Laura K. Westlund.

Designed by Lindsey Owens.
Main body text set in Avenir LT Pro. Typeface provided by Linotype AG.

Library of Congress Cataloging-in-Publication Data

Names: Eszterhas, Suzi, author, photographer.
Title: The adventures of Dr. sloth : Rebecca Cliffe and her quest to protect sloths / written and
    photographed by Suzi Eszterhas.
Description: Minneapolis : Millbrook Press, [2022] | Includes bibliographical references and index. |
    Audience: Ages 8–12 | Audience: Grades 4–6 | Summary: "Scientists know surprisingly little about
    sloths, but Becky Cliffe is working to change that. Visit the steamy jungles of Central and South America
    to see these adorable animals up close—and find out ways to protect them" —Provided by publisher.
Identifiers: LCCN 2021025226 (print) | LCCN 2021025227 (ebook) | ISBN 9781541589391 (library binding) |
    ISBN 9781728419022 (ebook)
Subjects: LCSH: Cliffe, Rebecca—Juvenile literature. | Sloths—Juvenile literature. | Sloths—Research—
    South America—Juvenile literature. | Sloths—Research—Central America—Juvenile literature. |
    Sloths—Conservation—Juvenile literature. | Zoologists—Great Britain—Biography—Juvenile literature.
Classification: LCC QL737.E2 E89 2022 (print) | LCC QL737.E2 (ebook) | DDC 599.3/13—dc23

LC record available at https://lccn.loc.gov/2021025226
LC ebook record available at https://lccn.loc.gov/2021025227

Manufactured in the United States of America
1-47473-48029-10/7/2021

SCAN THE
QR CODES
THROUGHOUT
THE BOOK TO
SEE SLOTHS iN
ACTION!

CONTENTS

INTRODUCTION
Meet Dr. Sloth

In my job as a wildlife photographer, I get to work with some amazing scientists around the world. On a trip to Costa Rica, I was lucky enough to meet Dr. Rebecca Cliffe, and now I'm very happy to introduce her to you.

Most people call Dr. Cliffe either Becky or Dr. Sloth. In the course of my trip, I spent many days with her in the jungle, observing the sloths high above us in the tree canopy. Together, we even got to see a three-toed sloth mother and newborn baby. The tiny baby stuck to her mother like glue. The mother crawled across the forest floor right in front of us, which was incredible to see!

Sloth Fact
A sloth baby is born with sharp teeth for eating leaves, claws for climbing, and eyes wide open. The baby stays with its mother until it is one year old.

See a baby sloth up close.
https://qrs.lernerbooks.com/babysloth

This is a wild sloth that humans named Esmerelda. I was so lucky to find her with her tiny baby, who was less than a week old.

Becky loves sloths more than anyone I know. While the sloths we were observing rested in the trees, she told me that there's still a lot that humans don't know about them. "Sloths are shy animals with very mysterious lives in the wild that scientists are only just starting to learn about and understand," Becky explained.

During that trip, Becky and I became fast friends. She told me about her dreams of working in sloth conservation. Of course, as a scientist, Becky wanted to continue to learn more about sloths, but she also wanted to find new ways to keep them safe. So we hatched a plan to continue working together so that I could photograph her journey to become the world's leading sloth conservationist.

Sloths move very slowly and spend a large part of their day resting. The hardest part about watching them is staying awake! Clearly, Becky (*bottom*), who snapped this selfie, is better at this than I am.

A Young Scientist

Becky at the age of five with her first furry friend, Bracken, her family's golden retriever

As a child in Preston, England, Becky didn't know what she wanted to be when she grew up. She did know that she loved animals of all sizes. She spent her days exploring the woods near her home, and one of her favorite activities was collecting insects. She would bring them home and observe them for a few days, and then release them.

When she was seven years old, Becky found a dead squirrel. She was concerned and curious. She wanted to know why the squirrel had died, so she brought it home to study. Though she never discovered what had happened to the squirrel, her attempt to figure it out was the beginning of her life as a scientist.

In school, Becky's favorite subject was biology, the study of living things. She studied hard and won first prize at an international science competition at the age of twelve. When she started college, Becky followed her passion for science and majored in zoology, the study of animals.

After college, Becky applied for a yearlong position to study sloths in Costa Rica. She had no idea that this would be the start of a lifelong love affair with these animals. She also never imagined that she would become one of the world's leading sloth experts. "It took a lot of hard work and courage to become a sloth scientist," said Becky. "Pursuing an unusual and adventurous career can be scary, but anything is possible if you put your mind to it."

ADS: from left, Tom Wooton, Jade Mroczak, Becky Cliffe, Rosalind Edwards and James Fairhu

team with chemistry

'ORTHAM'S Priory ology College was bub- ith success this week Year 8 team of pupils Chemical Egg competi- Liverpool John 's University. embers Tom Wootton,

Jade Mroczak, Becky Cliffe and James Fairhurst beat 20 other schools to win prizes for their school science depart- ment.
● Year 10 sudent Rosalind Ed- wards has been awarded a place on the prestigious

Salters Science Camp held over summer at the Univer of Manchester. Science teacher Mrs Carole Wynne said: "The competi for places is very high and has done very well to be giv place."

The local newspaper celebrated Becky's first scientific achievement. She and her team won first place in an international science competition. This was the first of many awards Becky would receive over the years.

One of Becky's favorite things about science is that you get to answer questions that no one else in the world knows the answers to!

Meet the Sloths

As I learned from Becky, sloths live only in Central and South America. But not all sloths are the same—scientists have identified six different species.

Some sloth species are two-fingered, and some species are three-fingered. Scientists used to describe sloths as being two-toed or three-toed, but in fact, all sloths have three toes on each of their rear feet. The difference is in their fingers.

The brown-throated three-fingered sloth is the most common species. They are found in Costa Rica and throughout Central and South America, from Honduras all the way down to Peru and Bolivia.

Pale-throated three-fingered sloths live in the northern part of South America, including French Guiana, Suriname, and Colombia. This species has a pale yellow patch of fur on its throat.

Brown-throated three-fingered sloth

Pale-throated three-fingered sloth

Maned three-fingered sloth

Maned three-fingered sloths are only found in the Atlantic coastal forest of Brazil. Each sloth in this species has a mane of black hair on its neck.

Pygmy three-fingered sloths are found only on one tiny, remote island in Panama. They are most famous for their swimming habits. Though all sloths can swim, these little sloths live in mangrove swamps and swim regularly. Pygmy, three-fingered sloths are some of the most critically endangered mammals in the world.

Pygmy three-fingered sloth

Linnaeus's two-fingered sloth

Hoffmann's two-fingered sloths are found in two distinct populations separated by the Andes Mountains. The northern population includes Costa Rica, and the southern population extends as far south as Brazil. These sloths have a more bearlike appearance and have long brown hair.

Linnaeus's two-fingered sloths live in many locations, including Venezuela, the Guianas, Colombia, Ecuador, Peru, and Brazil (north of the Amazon River). Despite how widespread they are, they're the sloth species scientists have studied the least.

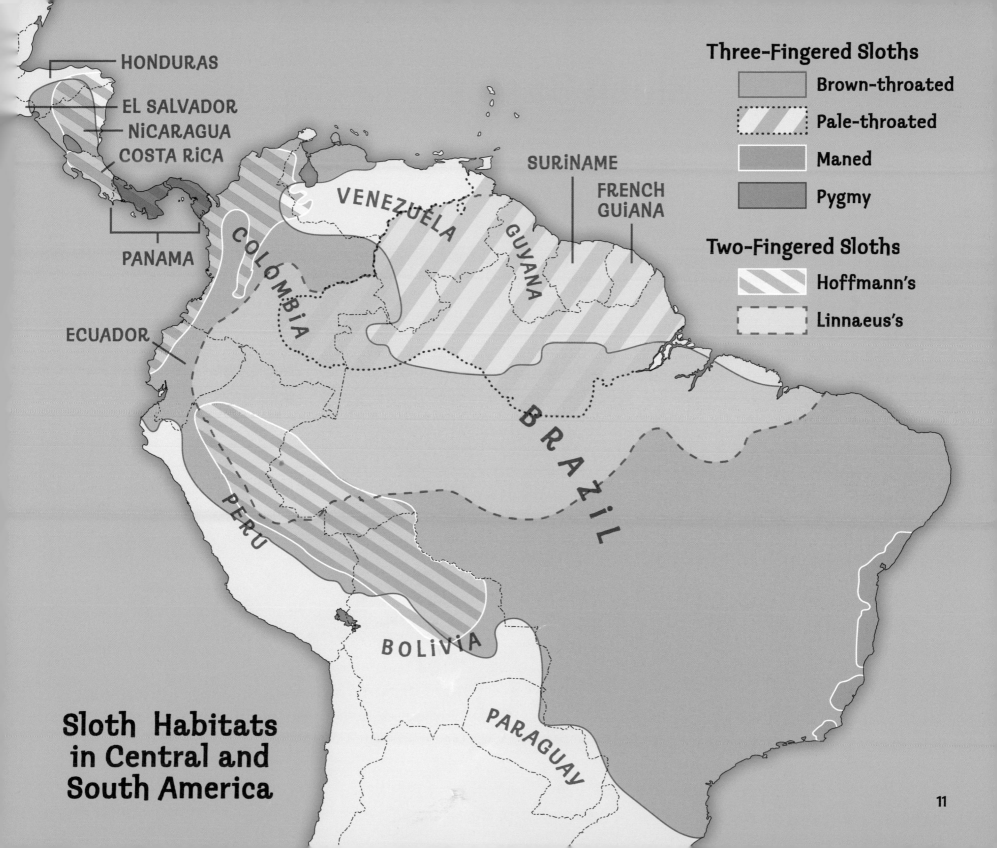

Three-Fingered Sloths

| | Brown-throated |
| Pale-throated |
| Maned |
| Pygmy |

Two-Fingered Sloths

| Hoffmann's |
| Linnaeus's |

HONDURAS
EL SALVADOR
NiCARAGUA
COSTA RiCA
PANAMA
ECUADOR

VENEZUELA
COLÓMBIA
SURiNAME
FRENCH GUiANA
GUYANA
BRAZiL
PERU
BOLiVIA
PARAGUAY

Sloth Habitats in Central and South America

Sloth Basics

Scientists are still working to learn more about sloths, but here is some of what we know about these mysterious creatures so far:

HABITAT
Sloths live in the tropical and cloud forests of Central and South America where the climate stays relatively warm year-round.

DIET
Three-fingered sloths are strict folivores and eat only leaves. Two-fingered sloths also eat mostly leaves but occasionally eat insects and fruit.

BEHAVIOR
As arboreal animals, sloths spend the majority of their time in trees. They are solitary, slow-moving, and active during the day or night. All sloths are territorial to some extent, but female three-fingered sloths hold the strongest territories, and male sloths will fight for access to the females.

BABIES
A baby sloth will stay with its mother for about twelve months. As well as drinking milk, the baby will begin to sample the leaves their mothers are feeding on from as early as one week old. This is how the mother teaches the baby which tree species are safe to eat. After weaning, the mother leaves her territory to her young and establishes a new territory elsewhere.

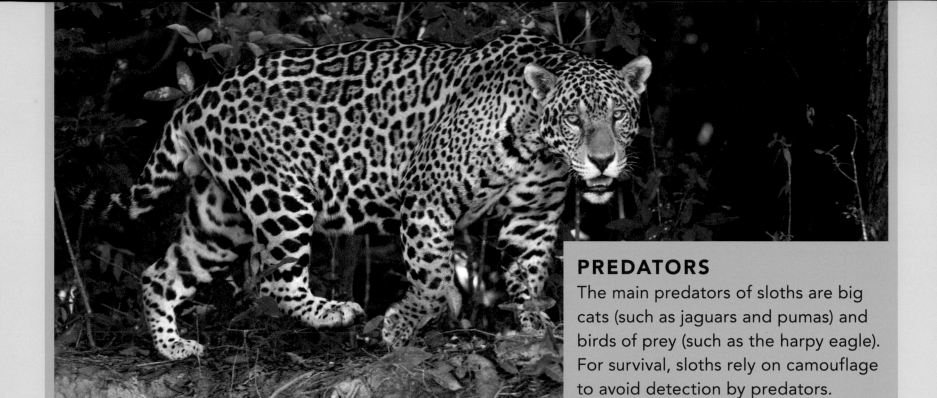

PREDATORS

The main predators of sloths are big cats (such as jaguars and pumas) and birds of prey (such as the harpy eagle). For survival, sloths rely on camouflage to avoid detection by predators.

HUMAN THREATS

Habitat loss due to development and agriculture poses the greatest threat to sloths. Power line electrocutions, dog attacks, and road collisions are also threatening sloths throughout their range.

LIFE SPAN

Scientists aren't sure of the life span of wild sloths. The oldest known two-fingered sloth is forty-six years old and lives at a zoo in Germany, while the oldest known three-fingered sloth died at the age of twenty-seven years old at a rescue center in Costa Rica.

Early Days with Sloths

Even early on, Becky had a hunch that a lot of what people thought they knew about sloths simply wasn't true. "People have thought for a long time that sloths just sleep all day, but I have always had a strong suspicion that a lot more happens when people aren't watching," said Becky. "I knew it would be difficult to prove, but understanding the secret lives of sloths became my mission."

For her first project as a sloth scientist, Becky observed sloths in a rescue center in Costa Rica. The rescue center was the perfect place to keep an eye on them all day long. Some of Becky's research included checking on sloths every four hours. For several months, she woke up in the middle of the night to do her "sloth rounds."

Sloth Fact

Sloths sleep for eight to ten hours a day. In comparison, koalas and lions regularly clock up to twenty hours.

Watch a baby sloth yawn!

https://qrs.lernerbooks.com/slothyawn

During this first study, Becky put special backpacks on the sloths. Inside the backpacks were tiny recording devices called daily diaries. Scientists have used daily diaries to record the activities of more than one hundred different animal species throughout the world. These animals include penguins, cheetahs, albatrosses, elephants, cormorants, and leopards. Becky was the first scientist to use them on sloths. She created a customized backpack harness to fit a sloth's body. That way, she could safely attach the devices to several different sloths at the center.

The backpacks recorded what the sloths were doing. Just as she had hypothesized, Becky discovered that sloths aren't lazy at all! In fact, they weren't even asleep during much of the time they were resting, and they slept only eight to ten hours per day. Sloths eat leaves, which don't offer many nutrients. As a result, sloths need to rest a lot to conserve energy, but for many of their resting hours they are wide awake.

This kind of research had never been done on three-fingered sloths before, so Becky's study was the first of its kind.

Becky discovered that a sloth's organs are attached to its ribs, which helps it breathe while hanging upside down. A sloth's anatomy helps prevent the lungs from being squashed and also helps it conserve energy.

Sloth Backpacks

After studying sloths at rescue centers, Becky decided to put backpacks on sloths in the wild. She spent days walking through the jungle in snake boots—special boots that protect against snakebites—while searching for wild sloths. Sloths are incredibly well camouflaged and blend right in with the forest vegetation. "Sloths can be almost impossible to spot," Becky explained. "My favorite sloth-spotting technique involves lying on the rain forest floor with a pair of good binoculars and carefully searching the canopy above me for any signs of fur."

It took Becky a while to learn how to spot sloths in the forest, but she's now an expert sloth spotter!

For her fieldwork, Becky has some special gear, including snake boots. Several species of venomous snakes live in Costa Rican rain forests, such as the fer-de-lance. Becky's hard, thick boots help to protect her from their dangerous bites!

Before attaching backpacks to wild sloths, Becky added a tracking device to the daily diary transmitter. Then she could follow where the sloths went. Becky studied the sloths for a wide range of time—some for weeks and months and others for up to three years! The backpack recorded information about when a sloth moved or ate, how high up the sloth was in the trees, which direction it was traveling, how much energy it was using, whether the sloth was in the sun or the shade, and the temperature of the air outside.

The tracking device in the sloth backpacks uses radiotelemetry. A radio transmitter inside the backpacks sends a silent signal to a special antenna Becky uses to determine their location.

Sloth Fact

A sloth's coloring allows it to blend in with the forest and virtually disappear. Its slow speed also helps it hide from predators. That's because sometimes a sloth moves so slowly that it's hard for predators to see the movement. Can you spot the sloth in this photograph?

Get another look at how a sloth blends in.

https://qrs.lernerbooks.com/slothcamouflage

Becky's study revealed many exciting things about sloths. She discovered that each sloth has a unique pattern of activity. Some woke up and fed at 3:00 a.m., while others woke up and fed at 3:00 p.m. Even with the same species, each individual sloth had a different activity schedule.

In the years that followed, Becky has continued studying sloths in Costa Rica. And she still uses backpacks with daily diaries to learn more and more about sloths' mysterious lives.

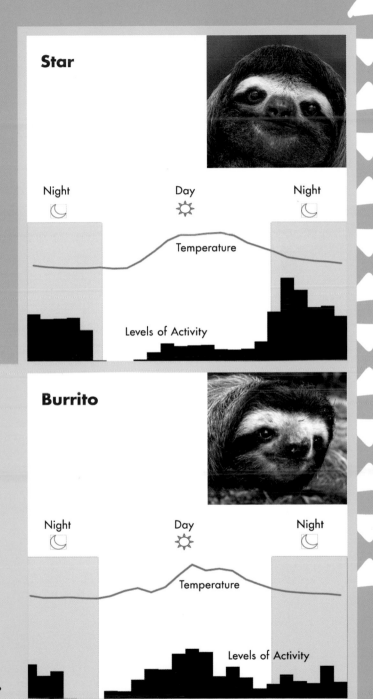

Star

Night · Day · Night

Temperature

Levels of Activity

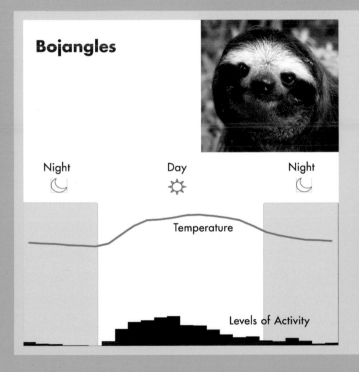

Bojangles

Night · Day · Night

Temperature

Levels of Activity

These three sloths were the stars of Becky's backpack project. Bojangles was fierce and skilled at hiding. Star was a sweet and gentle sloth who was easy to find in her favorite trees. Burrito was the first sloth to ever wear a backpack.

Burrito

Night · Day · Night

Temperature

Levels of Activity

Poo Dances and Digestion

Sloths are unique animals. Even the way they eliminate waste is different from any other animal on the planet. Sloths pee and poop only once a week. Slowly, they climb down from the tree canopy to the base of a tree. They dig a hole in the ground with their small tails, poop in the hole, then cover it. Becky calls this a "sloth poo dance."

Sloth Fact

Sloths come down to the ground to poop and pee. This is one way they mark their territory. When they poop, they poop a lot, usually losing about 30 percent of their body weight!

Watch a sloth climb to the ground with her baby.

https://qrs.lernerbooks.com/slothground

Sloths move slowly and awkwardly on the ground, which leaves them vulnerable to predators such as jaguars and pumas. This makes them very shy when they come down from the trees to poop. So Becky set up special camera traps that turn on and take pictures when they detect movement. But when she checked her traps, she found photos of lots of other animals but no sloths. After weeks and weeks of trying, she finally realized that sloths move so slowly that they don't even set off the traps!

Becky knew sloths ate leaves and she had seen them do their poo dance, but she wanted to know more about how a sloth's body digests the leaves. So she found a harmless red dye and fed it to sloths at rescue centers. Then she observed the sloths and studied their poop, specifically looking for the red dye. After thirty days she saw the dye. That's how she learned it takes a single leaf a month to move through a sloth's digestive system! Everything about a sloth is slow!

Three-fingered sloths are very picky eaters and eat only leaves from certain trees. They favor younger, greener leaves due to their lower toxin content but will also eat seedpods and flowers.

Every week Becky would trek through the forest to check her camera traps, which were strapped to the base of trees.

23

Sloth DNA

Along with studying sloth behavior and digestion, Becky was interested in how sloths inherit traits from their parents. To learn more about this, Becky needed to collect hair from various sloths. So she would climb a tree, capture a sloth, pluck out a few hairs, and then free the sloth again. Some sloths stayed very high in the trees, way out of her reach. Becky learned how to climb trees with safety ropes, a harness, and a helmet so that she could get close enough to catch them. Becky said, "Although sloths might look cute and cuddly, they are wild animals and can be very dangerous when scared! When I climb trees to collect hair samples from sloths I have to be careful to use all of the necessary safety equipment and to work quickly to minimize stress for the sloth."

After she obtained her samples, Becky ran tests on the sloth hair in a lab so she could find out more about sloth DNA and what traits are passed down from one sloth generation to the next. What's so important about DNA? It contains the instructions for how a living thing grows and functions, and it's passed down from parents to offspring.

Becky's genetic research took her to new heights! For this project, she climbed up to 100 feet (30 m) in the trees to find sloths.

Nearly every cell in a living thing contains DNA. Specific segments of DNA called genes determine or influence traits, including hair color and thickness. The tests showed that sloths who live in different regions and climates differ genetically. For example, sloths who live in colder, mountainous forests have genes that code for darker, thicker fur, which helps them to stay warm.

Becky also studied sloth babies that were born with missing fingers and toes, strangely shaped arms and legs, or undeveloped ears. More research needs to be done to find out why this happens. Becky suspects the reason may be linked to pesticides used on banana and pineapple plantations. She hopes that her research will help save sloths and keep their populations healthy.

Becky uses a tweezers to carefully pluck several strands of sloth hair.

This baby two-fingered sloth was born with only one finger. Rescue centers are receiving alarming numbers of baby sloths that have birth defects.

Sloth Fact

Different sloth species often have different colored fur. Some are blond to nearly white, while others are dark brown.

Check out a sloth's fur up close.

https://qrs.lernerbooks.com/slothcolor

Sloth Fur Surprises

One of the things that makes sloths so special is their fur. Amazingly, their fur is a habitat for other living things, including moths and beetles that aren't found anywhere else on Earth. Becky was fascinated by these creatures. "Everything in nature is interconnected," she explained. "I wanted to learn more about the sloths and the special species of moths and beetles that live in their fur so that I could better understand how these different species all impact each other's survival."

Sloth Fact

Scientists have found that some species of fungi and algae that grow in sloth fur may help the human body combat certain types of bacteria, parasites, and cancer.

Do you see the algae on this sloth?

https://qrs.lernerbooks.com/slothfur

For her research, Becky measured the size of male sloths' back patches as well as the body and arm length of the males. Becky hypothesized that bigger and stronger males have larger and brighter speculums.

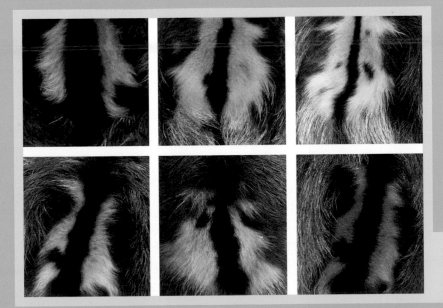

In this sample of six sloths, each back patch is unique.

Becky found that sloth moths spend their entire life in a sloth's fur, leaving only briefly to lay their eggs in sloth poop. The moths must quickly return to the sloth before the sloth's poo dance is over. Otherwise, they'll be stranded at the base of the tree. Becky also discovered that a single sloth can carry up to three hundred individual sloth moths!

In addition, sloths have more than eighty species of fungi and algae living in their fur. Each strand of sloth hair has cracks in it that allow algae to grow. The algae make the fur look green, providing camouflage for the sloth.

Becky observed that some male three-fingered sloths have a brightly colored patch of fur on their backs. The back patch, or speculum, is always yellow or orange with a black stripe down the center. Becky wanted to learn more about these patches, so she took pictures of them and drew them. She discovered that each male sloth had a completely unique back patch, much like a human fingerprint. She is still working to solve the mystery of why sloths have these back patches.

Sloth Bridges

Becky doesn't just study sloths. She also works hard to protect them. While most sloth species are not endangered, they are at risk because their habitats are being destroyed. Becky explained, "People are cutting down trees and destroying the rain forest habitat that sloths depend on because they want to use the land for things like cattle farming, agriculture, and new urban developments." So, Becky started the Sloth Conservation Foundation (SloCo), the world's only organization dedicated to saving sloths in the wild. SloCo is based in Costa Rica and is a team of fifteen sloth lovers working in sloth research and conservation.

Sloth Fact
The average speed of a sloth is 1 foot (0.3 m) per second when climbing.

Watch a sloth climb.
https://qrs.lernerbooks.com/slothclimb

Sloth crossing! In some areas where sloths live, signs warn drivers to keep an eye out for sloths crossing the road. Vehicles are one of the greatest threats to sloths.

In areas where humans have chopped down much of the forest, in order to find enough food to eat, sloths must climb down from the trees and cross busy roads to get from one patch of forest to the next. As you can imagine, they crawl slowly across roads, so they're at risk of being hit by fast-moving cars. To solve this problem, Becky's team created sloth crossing bridges in the trees at major crossing points.

Now sloths can safely use the ropes to cross over major traffic areas.

Sloths and other animals needed time to learn how to use the rope bridges. When most animals first see them, they're scared of the way the rope moves in the wind. Small mammals called kinkajous were the first to use the bridge. Monkeys followed a couple of months later, and sloths finally began trusting the rope after about six months.

Connecting Gardens

While bridges can help sloths safely cross from one patch of forest to another, the bridges alone aren't enough. Sloths also need large areas of forest to survive. So Becky plants native trees in rain forests where trees have been cut down. Every year her team plants five thousand sloth-friendly trees in gaps between forests. The team's goal is to reconnect patches of forests so sloths can travel easily while avoiding human dangers. As the trees grow, they will form a "forest corridor," so sloths can safely navigate from one patch of forest to the next.

These reforestation efforts aren't only good for the sloths—they also

Sloth Fact
In places like Costa Rica, sloths are "backyard wildlife." They're common in residential gardens with sloth-friendly trees!

Watch a sloth crawl along the ground.

https://qrs.lernerbooks.com/slothbackyard

provide a habitat for animals such as monkeys, tapirs, kinkajous, toucans, and macaws. And the forests benefit humans too. "Trees are not only important for sloths, but they are also essential for our survival as humans," said Becky. "They produce the oxygen that we breathe, stabilize the climate of our planet, regulate rainfall, and provide us with important medications. We need healthy rain forests for a healthy planet."

In addition to planting trees, Becky and her team encourage local farmers to grow cacao trees. The seeds of these plants are used to make chocolate. Farmers can plant cacao trees in the shade of the existing tree canopy, which means they can grow their crop without harming the forest. Other crops, such as bananas and pineapples, require farmers to cut down trees, so Becky tries to discourage farmers from growing them.

Did you know that sloths love chocolate? Sloths feed on the leaves and seeds of the cacao tree.

Patricio Mariano Silfeni takes care of tree seedlings the SloCo team planted to connect sloth habitat.

31

To the Rescue!

Becky started studying sloths nearly ten years ago. Since then, increasing numbers of orphaned and injured sloths have ended up at wildlife rescue centers. That's because there are more humans living and working in forest areas than ever before. This change means sloths are at greater risk of being hit by cars, attacked by dogs, or shocked by power lines.

Sometimes, a sloth baby loses its mother to human dangers and arrives at the center as an orphan. For example, a tree might be chopped down while the mother and baby are in it. When the tree falls, the mother's body protects the baby, but the mother may not survive. Then humans must intervene to raise the baby.

Sloths arrive at rescue centers every day—and in a variety of ways. Tourists found this injured sloth on the ground. They brought him to the rescue center on a bus.

An orphaned baby sloth clings to a plush toy sloth that resembles its mother. Generous sloth lovers from all over the world donate toys to help orphaned babies feel safe.

Sloth rescue centers work to help sloths and then release them back into the wild. Scientists are unsure what happens to orphaned sloths that rescue centers release. Sloth babies are born with some survival skills, but they also learn many behaviors from their mothers. For example, a sloth baby must learn which leaves are safe to eat and where to find them. Becky works with local rescue centers to monitor orphaned sloths after their release. "Making sure that orphaned sloths can have a second chance at a life in the wild is getting more and more important for the survival of the species," she explained. "As humans, it is very difficult for us to teach a baby sloth all of the survival skills that it needs, but with lots of care and attention I think it is possible."

Sloth Fact

From a very young age, mother sloths teach their babies which plants and leaves are safe to eat. Moms are the best teachers!

Watch a mom and baby share a leaf.
https://qrs.lernerbooks.com/slotheat

School Visits

Although Becky and her team are doing a lot to help sloths, they know that they need more help to keep sloths safe and healthy now and in the future. That's why Becky visits schools throughout Costa Rica to teach students about sloths and the importance of their habitat. "I tell children how much power we all have as individuals to protect our planet," she said. "Just by making small changes in our day-to-day habits, we can really make a big difference. One person at a time, one day at a time, and one choice at a time, we all have the ability to make a serious difference that will leave a lasting impact on the world."

Local children who live near sloths have a very important role to play in saving sloths. If local communities make changes to the way they live and think, then sloths and humans can live and thrive together in these jungle communities. For example, families can plant trees in their gardens to provide sloth-friendly habitat.

During visits, SloCo gives each student a booklet so that they can learn about sloths.

At the start of school visits, students often say negative, untrue things such as sloths are dirty or dangerous. But by the end, the children enthusiastically sign a pledge promising to protect and love sloths.

In most countries, it is against the law to own a pet sloth. When local police find a sloth being kept as a pet, they rescue it and bring it to a wildlife rehabilitation center. Whenever possible, a pet sloth is returned to the wild.

And if they see a sloth in trouble, they can call a local wildlife rescue center to help. Children who learn about sloths can talk to their parents and other family members about why it is important to protect them.

Another reason Becky's visits to schools are important is because some children are afraid of sloths and believe that they are very dangerous or gross animals. But children usually change their minds and become serious sloth lovers after listening to Becky talk about sloths!

Becky also helps students understand that sloths aren't meant to be pets. Most "pet sloths" are unjustly taken from the wild. They become traumatized and scared of living in a cage. And properly caring for a sloth is very difficult. Sloths in captivity will die without the care of a wildlife expert.

Sloth Fact

Sloths don't show stress the way other animals do. Their natural response to fear is to hold still, so it is difficult to tell when a sloth is scared or stressed.

See Becky carry a sloth in the rain forest.

https://qrs.lernerbooks.com/slothstill

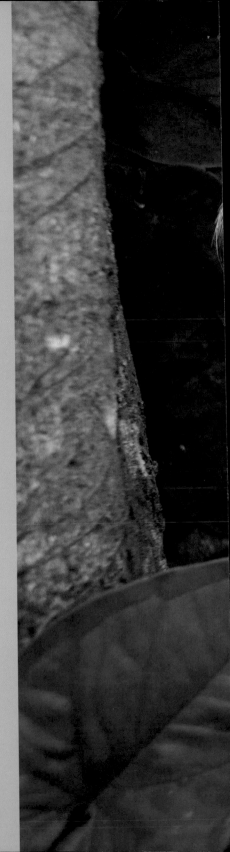

CONCLUSiON
How Can You Help Sloths?

You don't have to be a scientist or live in Costa Rica to be a friend to sloths. Here are some ways to help these gentle, fascinating creatures no matter where you live:

- Hold your own bake sale or other fundraiser. Donate the money you raise to an organization that helps sloths, such as the Sloth Conservation Foundation.

- Learn as much as you can about sloths. Then tell your friends and family about why sloths need our help.

- Bring this book to your classroom, and share it with your friends. Or create a presentation about sloths to educate your classmates.

- Make art that features sloths, and display it where others can see it. Encourage people to ask questions, and then tell them what you know!

- Ask your parents to buy local, organic produce. Many fruit plantations in South and Central America use pesticides that are harmful to sloths.

- If you travel to places where sloths live, avoid taking selfies with sloths or other wild animals. If you see a wild sloth, keep your distance and give it at least 15 feet [4.6 m] of safe space. As a solitary prey species, they enjoy lots of personal space and become stressed out if anyone gets too close.

GLOSSARY

agriculture: the practice of farming, including producing crops and raising livestock

anatomy: the physical structure of an organism or any of its body parts

arboreal: living in or frequently found in trees

biology: the study of living things, including plants, animals, and other organisms

birth defect: a structural change present at birth that can affect almost any part of the body

camouflage: hiding or disguising something by covering it up or changing its appearance to look like its environment

cloud forest: a type of rain forest that is between 3,000 and 8,000 feet (1,000 and 2,500 m) in altitude and is characterized by many epiphytes, plants that live on other plants and take moisture and nutrients from the air. Cloud forests have an abundance of mist and fog.

DNA (deoxyribonucleic acid): the material that carries all the information a living thing needs to grow and function

folivore: an animal that feeds on leaves

gene: a part of DNA that contains information to make proteins that control various bodily traits or the function of other genes

genetic: of or relating to genes; caused or controlled by inherited genes

habitat: the place or type of environment where a living thing naturally lives or grows

hypothesis: an idea that proposes a tentative explanation for something a scientist has observed. A scientist will conduct experiments to test a hypothesis and determine whether it is correct.

monitor: to watch, observe, or look after

organ: a part of a living thing that is specialized to do a particular task in the body; consists of cells and tissues

organic: grown without the use of human-made substances, such as fertilizers, antibiotics, or pesticides

organism: a living thing made up of one or more cells and able to carry on the activities necessary for life

pesticide: a human-made substance used to get rid of pests, such as bugs, on plants

predator: an animal that survives by killing and eating other animals

radiotelemetry: using a radio to transmit data to another device

solitary: growing or living alone

species: a category of living things that is made up of related living things that have similar traits and are able to produce offspring together

speculum: a sloth's back patch, a unique patch of yellow or orange fur with a black stripe on a male sloth's back

territory: an area that is occupied and defended by an animal or group of animals

transmitter: a device that sends radio or television signals to another device

tree canopy: the uppermost leaf layer of a tree that acts as a shade or shelter by hanging over the ground

wean: to get a young animal used to food other than its mother's milk

FURTHER READING AND WEBSITES

Books

Delacre, Lulu. *¡Olinguito, de la A la Z! Descubriendo El Bosque Nublado / Olinguito, from A to Z! Unveiling the Cloud Forest.* New York: Children's Book Press, 2016. Discover Ecuador's cloud forest with lyrical text in both English and Spanish and realistic illustrations.

Foley, Erin. *Costa Rica.* New York: Cavendish Square, 2017. Take an in-depth look at Costa Rica in this book, which covers the economy, geography, history, environment, food, festivals, and more.

Gregory, Josh. *Sloths.* New York: Children's Press, 2016. Learn about the sloth life cycle, and find out lots of facts about sloths in this photo book.

Websites/Videos

The Sloth Conservation Foundation
https://slothconservation.org/
Find out more about the organization Rebecca Cliffe founded, including information about its current projects, such as connected gardens, sloth crossings, sloth-friendly tourism, and more.

Walking through the Amazing Monteverde Cloud Forest, Costa Rica
https://youtu.be/kIwB7J_wtEI
Check out video footage from a guided tour of the Monteverde Cloud Forest, highlighting what makes this location so special.

Why Are Sloths So Slow? And Other Sloth Facts
https://nationalzoo.si.edu/animals/news/why-are-sloths -so-slow-and-other-sloth-facts
The Smithsonian's National Zoo site has facts about and photos of sloths.

INDEX